Folded Fabric

Elegance

Rami Kim

American Quilter's Society
P. O. Box 3290 • Paducah, KY 42002-3290
www.AmericanQuilter.com

Located in Paducah, Kentucky, the American Quilter's Society (AQS) is dedicated to promoting the accomplishments of today's quilters. Through its publications and events, AQS strives to honor today's quiltmakers and their work and to inspire future creativity and innovation in quiltmaking.

EXECUTIVE EDITOR: NICOLE C. CHAMBERS
EDITOR: AARON CHAMBERS
GRAPHIC DESIGN: ELAINE WILSON & AMY CHASE
COVER DESIGN: MICHAEL BUCKINGHAM
PHOTOGRAPHY: CHARLES R. LYNCH

Special thanks to models Kelly Dowdy, Cindy Pugh, and Suzanne Spiceland and to Kay Smith, Caryl Bryer Fallert, and Dwain Smith & Margie Cissell of the Cissell-Smith House for use of their homes.

Library of Congress Cataloging-in-Publication Data

Kim, Rami.

Folded fabric elegance / by Rami Kim.

p. cm.

Summary: "Three-dimensional, traditional Korean folding techniques for quilting. Meticulously illustrated and executed. Includes American smocking, harlequin tucks, and pinwheels. Projects include wallhangings, pillows, purses, totes, and chargers. Finishing instructions included"--Provided by publisher.

ISBN 978-1-57432-941-4

1. Patchwork--Patterns. 2. Quilting--Patterns. I. Title.

TT835.K48866 2007

746.4609519--dc22

2007034659

Additional copies of this book may be ordered from the American Quilter's Society, PO Box 3290, Paducah, KY 42002-3290, or online at www.AmericanQuilter.com. For phone orders only 800-626-5420. For all other inquiries, call 270-898-7903.

Proudly printed and bound in the United States of America

This book is dedicated to my Lord, Jesus.

Acknowledgments

I want to give many thanks to our mothers and grandmothers who endeavored to show us lucky daughters the beauties of the world and the fun of paper folding. My adventure began by sewing Barbie® clothes for my two beautiful daughters, Deanna and Chelsey Lee, who are now intelligent teenagers. When I started my journey by studying biochemistry and molecular endocrinology with studies in the genetic engineering field, I had no idea that I would end up writing a book about fabric art, traveling to many places, lecturing, and teaching my works.

I sincerely appreciate the opportunities God has given me, all these chances to make wonderful friends through quilting and sewing. Even if I cannot mention every single name, I want you ladies to know that you are always in my thoughts.

I especially want to thank my husband, Ki-hyeok Lee, M.D., for his love, support, and patience, even through the temper tantrums during my so-called "creative periods;" my loving husband who still asks me whether I miss my research lab or not. You know my answer already: "No, no, no…"

I also want to praise the following people because of their guidance and assistance for the better or the worse:

Susan Simpson Berbec ~ Without you, this book would be an impossible dream. You gave me timely encouragements when I was utterly discouraged. In addition, you eloquently first-edited my manuscript and you loved me as your friend no matter what mistakes I made.

My family ~ My husband and my two wonderful daughters, Deanna and Chelsey Lee, who are always willing to help me; my loving mom and dad (In Joon Kim and Yong Ju Kim); my parents-in-law (Kyong Hee Lee and Hee Soon Lee, the best in the world); my aunt, Il Joon Lee, for always being there to listen and comment on my crazy ideas; my brother Wooil Kim for supplying continuous entertainment; and all other family members who find a place in my heart.

Church ~ Pastor Han and my church family who pray for me twenty-four seven

My friends ~ There is an endless list of names, but you know how much I appreciate your friendships. Wherever you are, I hope everything is flowing smoothly.

Special thanks to Meissner's Sewing Center, Triad Plus, Cabin Fever Quilt Shoppe, Superior Threads, Hobb's Bonded Fiber, and Bernina of America for ongoing sustenance during my journey as a fabric artist.

AQS editor Nicole Chambers for her gracious advice on creating this book, and all of my special friends at American Quilter's Society and Schroeder Publishing Co., Inc.

God bless you all,

Rami Kim

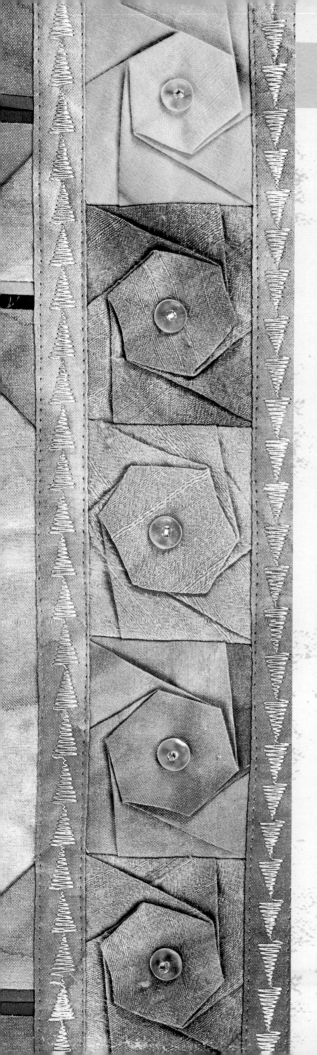

Contents

Introduction

Chopkey, the Korean form of paper folding, traces its origins back to the Kokuryo and Shilla Dynasties. For more than 1500 years, this art has been passed from one generation to the next. I still recall those happy childhood hours spent at my grandmother's table as we folded colorful cranes, frogs, baskets, and flowers.

There is a nearly unlimited potential in transforming a two-dimensional material into the fantastic three dimensions of life. The variety of colors and shapes can make an ordinary house as vivid and wonderful as a childhood daydream.

Chopkey, however, is not just about the finished piece. Rather, one enjoys the entire process, from formulating the design to selecting the materials to displaying the finished creation. Like the best things of this world, Chopkey forces us to enjoy not just our successes, but also the vivacity of living. Chopkey is an excellent mental exercise. It enhances our creativity and cultivates our artistic impulses. It enhances hand-eye coordination and develops fine motor skills.

Whether I see a mother and her child at work on a project or an elderly couple learning a new technique, I am reminded of the many sides of life, the glory of creating something new, the necessity of learning, and the warmth of accomplishment. Perhaps most importantly, I am reminded that every project (like life) turns out differently than its original design.

Like most Korean children, I learned Chopkey at an early age from my grandmother and mother. For many years, I have entertained the idea of connecting Chopkey to my grown-up passion of designing wearable art. Finally, memories of those special times spent with my mother combined with my love of fabric inspired me to apply these folding techniques to my designs. I found that the addition of Chopkey brought a whole new dimension (literally) and Asian flair to my wearable art. I hope you enjoy adult-style Chopkey and that it brings you many fond memories. Please remember to slow down and enjoy the entire process.

The lotus blooms elegantly along the surface of clean water, even as its roots are planted in the muddy bottom of its pond. Revered throughout Asian culture for its beauty as well as its resilience, the lotus blossom has come to symbolize a spiritual purity separate from the world of secular worries.

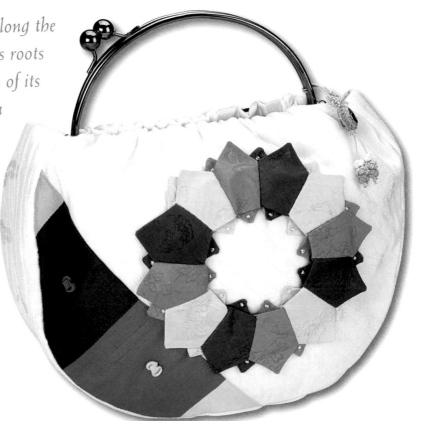

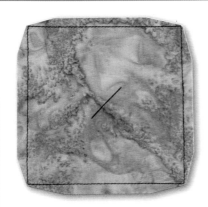

To make one flower with twelve petals, cut twenty-four 3½" fabric squares. (Or any size you prefer.)

1. Pair two squares right sides together. Sew completely around the paired squares using a ¼" seam allowance. Trim away the excess fabric in the corners. Cut a 1" slit on the diagonal through only the inside layer of fabric.

2. Turn the square right side out through the slit and press. Orient the square on your work surface on point so that the slit faces up and runs from left to right. Fold the square in half by bringing the bottom corner to the top corner. Press the folded edge. The slit will be along the inside fold. Take the recently folded corner and align it back over the biased edge, as seen in the photo. The point should extend ¼" beyond the bottom fold. Press.

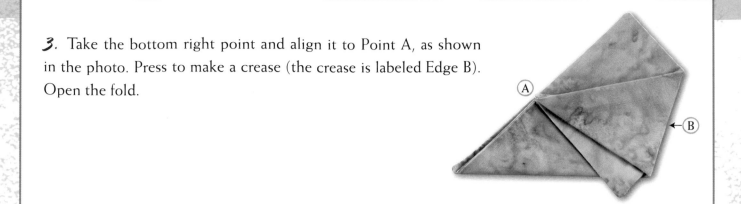

3. Take the bottom right point and align it to Point A, as shown in the photo. Press to make a crease (the crease is labeled Edge B). Open the fold.

4. Take the bottom left point and align it to Point C, as shown in the photo. Press to make a crease (the crease is labeled Edge D). Open the fold.

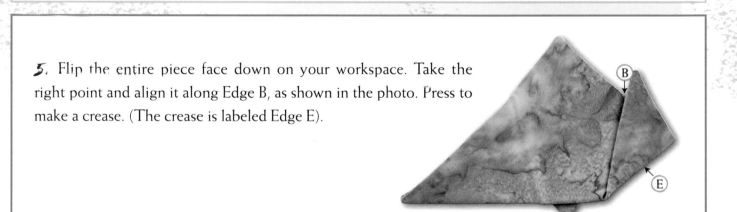

5. Flip the entire piece face down on your workspace. Take the right point and align it along Edge B, as shown in the photo. Press to make a crease. (The crease is labeled Edge E).

6. Take the left point and align it along Edge D. Press to make a crease. (The crease is labeled Edge F).

7. Open the folds as shown.

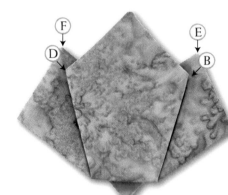

8. Grasping the points of the top triangle only, fold Edge E under Edge B and Edge F under Edge D. Congratulations! You have finished one petal. To complete the lotus blossom, make a total of twelve petals.

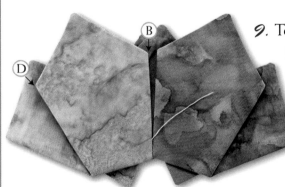

9. To connect the petals align Edge B of one petal with Edge D of another. Connect using either a whipstitch or ladder stitch.

10. Flip the stitched petals over and tack stitch two adjacent petals together as shown. (Match the color of thread and hide knots and tails properly.) Repeat this step until all twelve petals have been joined to form a circle.

Mount the assembled flower on background fabric by using beads at the points. Attach the beads by sewing through all the layers. (Refer to page 35.) ◆

The Hexagon Chopkey adds an irresistible three-dimensional texture to your projects that just cannot be found with any flat border. It is perfect for quilts and wearables, but I especially love using this Chopkey on handbags. Make the Hexagon Chopkey the finishing touch of your next project.

1. Cut one large and one small hexagon using the template found on page 49. I recommend using a tone-on-tone or solid fabric to better showcase the folds. Use a fashion fabric for the large hexagon and muslin for the small hexagon.

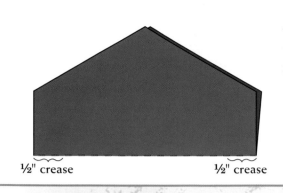

2. Fold the large hexagon in half wrong sides together and points matching. Pinch both edges along the fold to make ½" long creases, as shown in the illustration.

½" crease   ½" crease

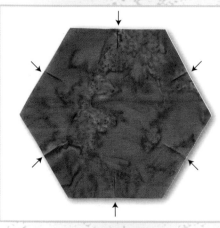

3. Fold the hexagon in half, wrong sides together and points matching, two additional times so that each point has been paired. Pinch the edges with each fold so that the hexagon will have six ½" creases, as shown in the photo.

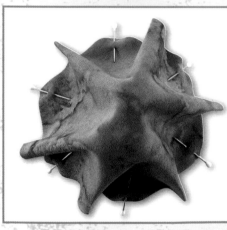

4. Place the large hexagon on top of the small hexagon, wrong sides together. Pin each corner of the large hexagon to its corresponding corner of the small hexagon.

5. Using a pinch between your thumb and forefinger, make a pleat to the right of the pinch, and pin the tuck to the small hexagon. Pinch and pleat all six sides. To form a hexagon in the middle, you will need to rotate and pat down the center at the same time.

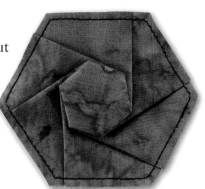

6. Baste along all edges using a ⅛" seam allowance. Press but do not iron.

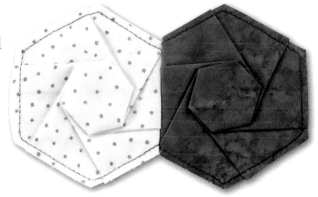

7. Connect hexagons until the strip is the desired length. Sew the row together using a ¼" seam allowance. Press seams open.

Align your ruler along the inside corners and trim off the pointed sides with a rotary cutter.

8. Cut two 1" strips across the width of your fabric. Fold under ¼" along both long sides of each strip. To simplify this step, you can use a ½" bias tape maker.

Topstitch these strips to your Hexagon Chopkey ¼" from the raw edge. ✦

This folded flower has always looked to me like the famous tulips from the Netherlands. As a result (and because this is my book), I have christened this Chopkey the Asheeya Tulip.

FOLDING A TULIP

Cut two identical squares of your choosing.

	Flower	*Leaf*
Small	3½"	2¾"
Medium	4"	3"
Large	4½"	3½"

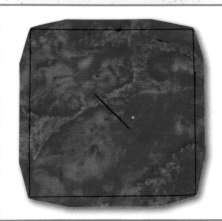

1. Pair the squares right sides together. Sew completely around the paired squares using a ¼" seam allowance. Trim away the excess fabric in the corners. Cut a 1" slit on the diagonal through only the inside layer of fabric, as shown in the photo.

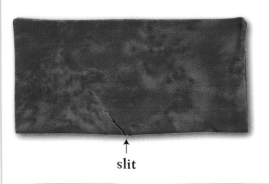

↑
slit

2. Turn the square right side out through the slit and press. Orient the square so that the slit faces the table. Fold the square in half to form a rectangle, as shown in the photo. Press to form a sharp crease. Open the piece.

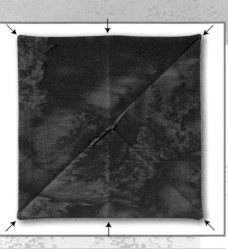

3. With the slit facing up, fold the piece diagonally so that the points match, press creases and open. Fold diagonally in the other direction so that the two remaining points match. Your piece now has a horizontal crease and two diagonal creases.

4. Orient the piece with the slit facing down and the horizontal crease running parallel to your workspace. Grasp the corners of the horizontal crease and push together and down creating a triangle.

5. Fold the Tulip points up in an overlaying fashion, as shown in the photos.

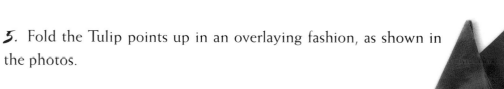

아시아튤립

Cut two identical squares of your choosing.

	Flower	Leaf
Small	3½"	2¾"
Medium	4"	3"
Large	4½"	3½"

FOLDING THE LEAVES

1. Pair two squares right sides together. Sew completely around the perimeter using a ¼" seam allowance. Trim away the excess fabric in the corners. Cut a 1" slit on the diagonal through the inside layer of fabric.

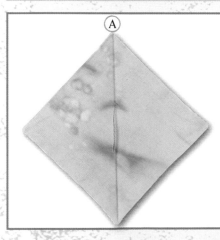

2. With the slit positioned up, fold the square in half diagonally following the direction of the slit. Press to form a crease (labeled Edge A). Open the fold.

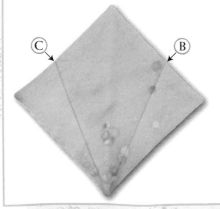

3. Position the piece like a diamond, with the slit facing down.

First, fold the left corner so that its edge touches Edge A. Press to form Edge B and open the fold.

Align the right corner so that its edge aligns along Edge A. Press to form Edge C and open the fold.

4. With the slit facing up, fold the left corner so that crease edge B is aligned with crease A. Press to form edge D and open the fold.

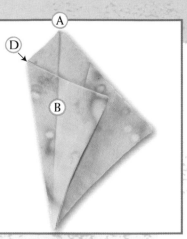

Fold the right corner so that crease C is aligned with crease A. Press to form edge E and open the fold.

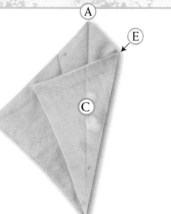

You now have five creases that fan out like the sun.

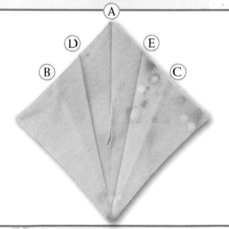

5. With the slit facing up, fold the newly formed Edges B and C toward the center so that they align along Edge A. ✦

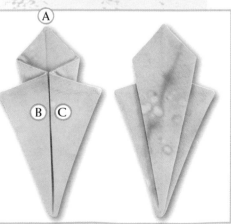

Chopkey 4 ~ *Lightning Bug*

Traditionally called a bat (an auspicious sign in Korean culture), I have renamed this ornament the lightning bug as it reminds me of one special summer evening walk, when out of nowhere lightning bugs came swooping across the darkened sky. A very lucky sign, I thought. I hope these lightning bugs bring you happiness and love.

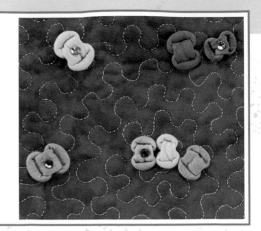

Fabric square size	Bug size
2" square	½" bug
2½" square	⅝" bug
2¾" square	¾" bug
3¼" square	⅞" bug

Use fabric that looks the same on both front and back, such as batik cotton, since both sides will show on the finished bug.

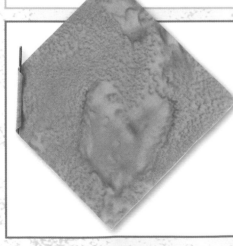

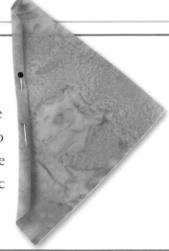

1. Cut a square of fabric the size of your choosing. Position the piece like a diamond along your work surface. Use a large tapestry needle to roll your left corner to the center, as shown in the photo. Remove the tapestry needle and pin the rolled fabric in place.

2. Using the tapestry needle again, roll the right corner to the center until the rolls meet in the center. Reposition the pin to temporarily hold both rolls.

3. Remove the pin holding the rolls. Fold the piece in half so that the crease between the rolls faces outward. Wrap basting thread snugly around the tube about one third of the way towards the raw edge, as shown in the photo. Make a knot and trim the loose thread end.

4. Cut the piece ⅛" below the thread wrap, as shown in the photo, and discard the two tails.

5. Using your thumbnails, grab the edges of each roll and spread them outward like a blooming flower.

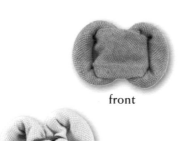

front

back

6. Use fabric glue to stick the bugs to the surface of your project. Using matching thread, appliqué around the perimeter of each bug. ✦

Continuous prairie points lend themselves to bead and crystal embellishments, which could add just the right flourish to your next quilt border or garment. Any resemblance to the traditional prairie point is purely coincidental.

Squares 2" x 2" work well for garments and accessories. For quilt borders and home décor projects, I recommend 3" to 4" squares.

FOLDING CONTINUOUS PRAIRIE POINTS

1. Use a permanent marker with an ultra-fine point to draw the prairie point grid on wrong side of the fabric, as shown in the illustration. Be sure to draw the bottom row first.

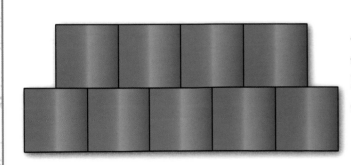

2. Next draw the top row. Start your first square in the middle of the first bottom square. Remember, the top row is always one-half square shorter on each end.

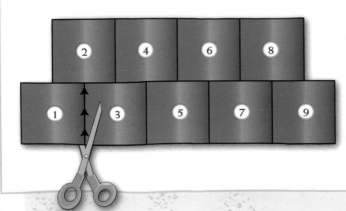

3. Cut out the double row of squares along the outside lines. Then cut each vertical line, starting from the outer edge to the center line.

4. Take Square 1, as labeled in the photo. Fold the bottom left corner (marked Point C) diagonally to meet the top right corner (marked Point B). Press along the diagonal fold.

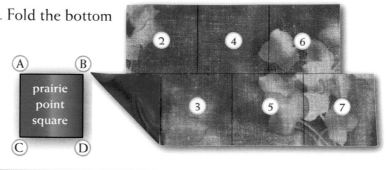

5. Still grasping Square 1, fold Point D diagonally to meet Point A, as shown in the photo. Press along the diagonal fold.

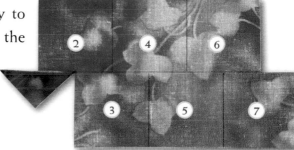

6. Take Square 2 and fold Point A diagonally to meet Point D, as shown in the photo. Press along the diagonal fold.

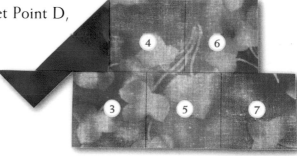

7. Take Square 1 again and fold it up, across the horizontal center line, as shown in the photo. Square 1 is now a triangle with its point facing up.

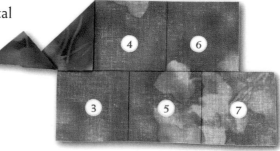

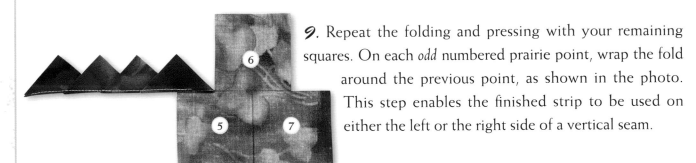

8. Take Square 2 and fold Point B diagonally to meet C. Press along the fold. It will overlap Square 1, as shown in the photo. Your piece now has two mountain peaks.

9. Repeat the folding and pressing with your remaining squares. On each *odd* numbered prairie point, wrap the fold around the previous point, as shown in the photo. This step enables the finished strip to be used on either the left or the right side of a vertical seam.

10. When the entire strip has been folded into prairie points, pin through all the fabric layers at each *valley*. Baste the layers together ⅛" from the raw edge.

11. Sew the prairie point strip between two pieces of fabric using a ¼" seam allowance. To embellish the strip, poke your finger into the first prairie point and spread it open. Add a bead or any other embellishment in the center by stitching through all the layers. ✦

Prairie Point Tips

When you sew a strip on the right side of a vertical seam, be sure that the peaks point to the right and the open folds face upward.

To make a mirror image, sew your next strip so that the peaks point to the left and the open folds face upward.

right-sided   left-sided

For prairie point strips that are not inserted into a seam, you can cover the raw edges with a 1" bias strip folded under ¼" along both long sides of the strip. To simplify folding, you can use a ½" bias tape maker. Topstitch the strip in place where desired.

1. Cut a piece of fabric 2½ times larger than the desired width and length of your finished smocked piece (for ½" grid dots).

Mark a grid of dots on the wrong side of your fabric. A good starting place is ½" grid for wearable art and bags. Use a 1" grid for larger projects.

Mark arrows above every other column to indicate the starting place for each column of stitching.

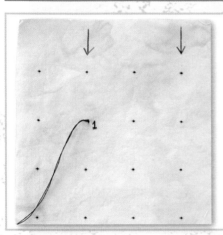

2. Thread your needle with a double strand of regular thread or a single thread of heavy-duty sewing thread. Use a color that closely matches your fabric.

Insert the needle into the right-hand side of Dot 1 and bring the needle out through the left-hand side of the same dot, taking a tiny stitch.

To create this texture, you need to work in columns.

● The red Dot 1 is the starting point for each column.

↔〰〰〰➤ The squiggly arrows indicate where the thread is pulled snug and dots overlap each other.

——— The straight lines in each column indicate where the thread and fabric remain flat.

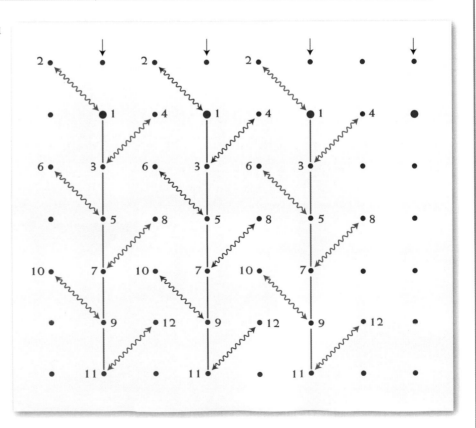

3. Pick up Dot 2. Return and pick up Dot 1 again. Pull Dots 1 and 2 together to form a pleat. Knot securely. Keep in mind that all dots are picked up this way and that the thread is carried from dot to dot on the wrong side of the fabric.

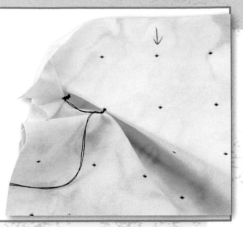

4. Pull the thread through, leaving a long straight stitch between Dots 1 and 3. **Do not pull this stitch tight.** With the thread looped above the needle, slip the needle under the thread between Dots 1 and 3 and over the thread loop.

Pull the thread tight at Dot 3 to form a knot. Be sure to keep the fabric flat between Dots 1 and 3.

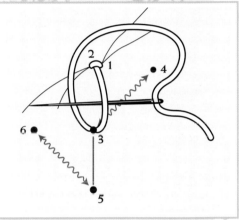

5. Pick up Dot 4. Return and pick up Dot 3. Pull Dots 3 and 4 together to form a pleat then knot securely. Pick up Dot 5.

6. Slip the needle under the thread between Dots 3 and 5 and over the thread loop (just as you did with Dots 1 and 3). Make a knot at Dot 5. Continue the column in this manner.

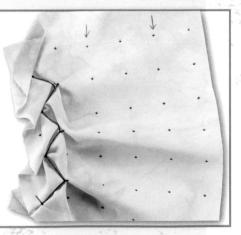

7. Once this column is completed, find the next column marked with an arrow and begin again. Stitch all columns in this manner. When finished, the wrong side will look like the photo. ✦

1. To calculate the size of fabric piece to cut, multiply the desired **length** of the finished piece by 1.5 then add a 4" allowance. Multiply the desired **width** of the finished piece by 2 then add a 4" allowance.

For instance, if an 8" (l) x 8" (w) piece was desired, a 16" (l) x 20" (w) piece would be cut.

Mark a grid on the wrong side of your fabric, as shown in the illustration.

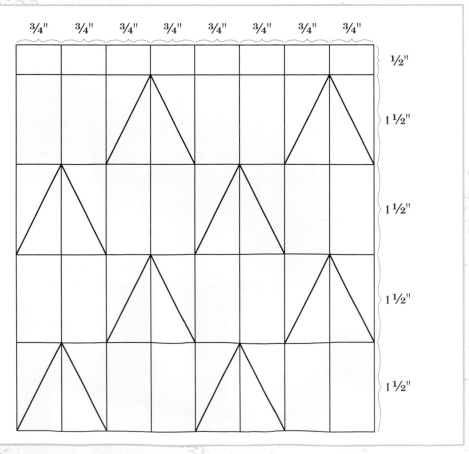

2. To create this texture you can use a sewing machine, unless you prefer to hand stitch. Thread the machine top and bottom with matching color thread. With wrong sides together, hold together Line AC and Line BC. Edge stitch along the folds using a ¹⁄₁₆" seam allowance. Backstitch the beginning and ending segments.

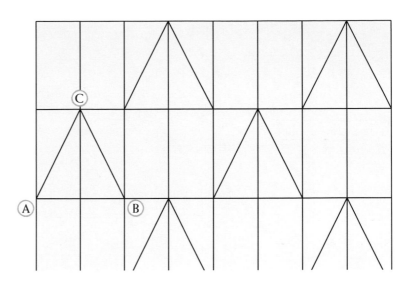

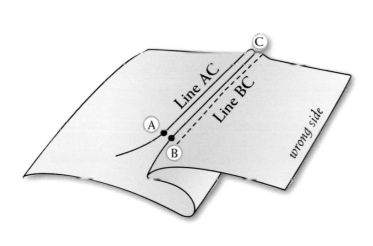

3. Repeat by stitching together each subsequent section with marked diagonal lines. ✦

back side

front side

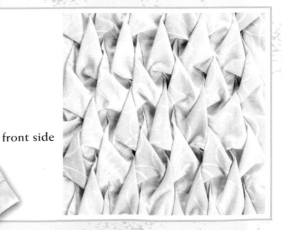

1. To calculate the appropriate **width** of fabric piece to cut, multiply the needed size by 2 and then add 4" to the that measurement. To calculate the appropriate **length**, add 4" to the finished size needed (for a ½" grid of dots).

For example, if an 8" (w) x 8" (l) finished piece was desired, a 20" (w) x 12" (l) piece would be cut.

Mark a ½" grid of dots on the wrong side of your fabric, as shown in the illustration. Counting rows from 1 to 4, mark an arrow on every 1st and 4th row, as shown. These arrows indicate the starting place of a new row for smocking.

To create this texture, you need to work in rows.

● The red Dot 1 is the starting point for each column.

∼∼∼▶ The squiggly arrows indicate where the thread is pulled snug and dots overlap each other.

——— The straight lines in each row indicate where the thread and fabric remain flat.

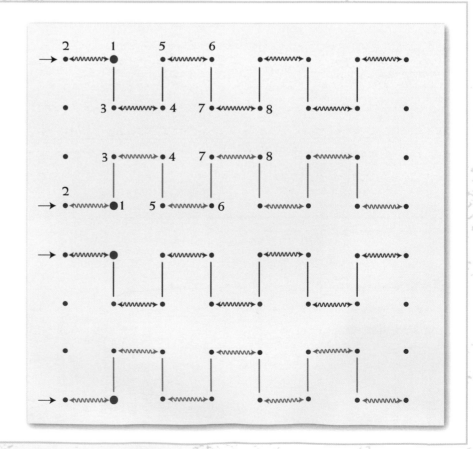

2. Thread your needle with a double strand of regular thread or a single thread of heavy-duty sewing thread. Use a color that closely matches your fabric. All work is done on the wrong side of the fabric. Insert the needle into the right-hand side of Dot 1 and bring the needle out through the left-hand side of the same dot, taking a tiny stitch.

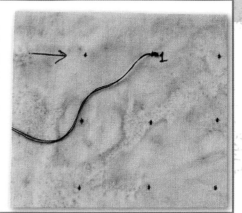

3. Keep in mind that all dots are picked up this way and that the thread is carried from dot to dot on the wrong side of the fabric. Pick up Dot 2. Return to pick up Dot 1 again.

Pull together Dots 1 and 2 in order to form a pleat. Knot securely.

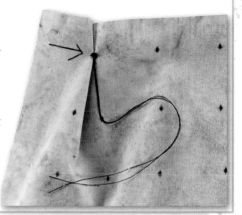

4. Pick up Dot 3. Pull the thread through, leaving a long straight stitch between Dots 1 and 3. Do not pull this stitch tight. With the thread looped above the needle, slip the needle under the thread between Dots 1 and 3 and over the thread loop.

Pull the thread snug at Dot 3 to form a knot. Be sure to keep the fabric flat between Dots 1 and 3.

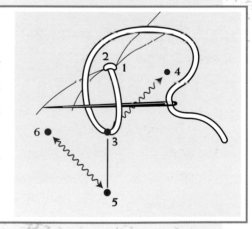

5. Pick up Dot 4. Return and pick up Dot 3.

Pull Dots 3 and 4 together to form a pleat then knot securely.

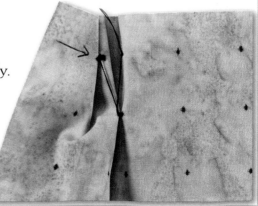

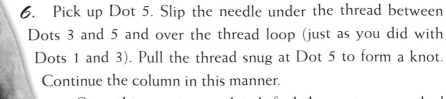

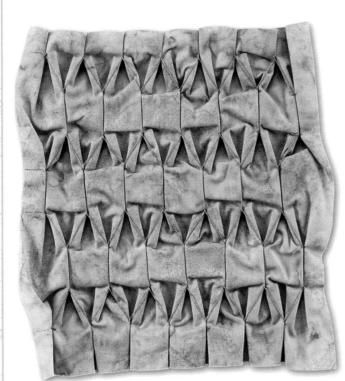

6. Pick up Dot 5. Slip the needle under the thread between Dots 3 and 5 and over the thread loop (just as you did with Dots 1 and 3). Pull the thread snug at Dot 5 to form a knot. Continue the column in this manner.

Once this row is completed, find the next row marked with an arrow and begin again. Stitch all rows in this manner. ✦

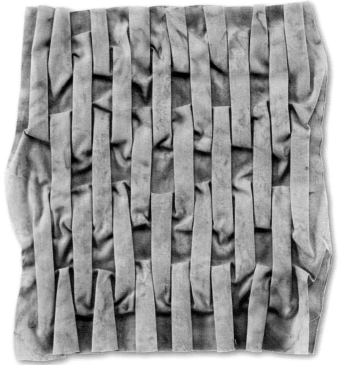

back side

front side
(press folds flat to get this shape)

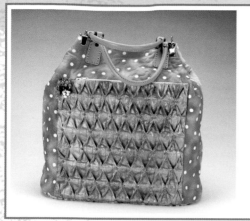

Harlequin Tucks can add sumptuous texture and a new dimension to your next project. I recommend a tone-on-tone or a solid fabric for this technique. A busy print will not adequately showcase the beauty of these enchanting folds. For something really special, embellish these tucks with sparkling beads.

Sewing Harlequin Tucks

1. To calculate the required size of fabric, double the **width** of your desired finished product, and add 3". Then add 3" to the **length** of the finished piece. For example, if you wanted an 8" (w) x 8" (l) piece, you would cut a 19" x 11" rectangle.

Use an erasable marker, such as chalk, to mark horizontal lines spaced 1" apart, across the right side of your cut fabric.

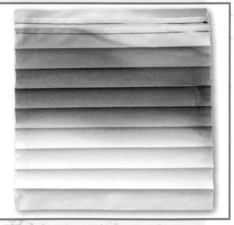

2. With the right side facing up, fold the fabric (with the wrong sides together) at the first marked line and then press to crease. Open the fold. Fold and press each subsequent line.

Using your ¼" foot, sew each tuck by running the edge of your foot precisely along each fold. Because the top and bottom threads will show, decorative thread is recommended.

Press all the tucks in one direction.

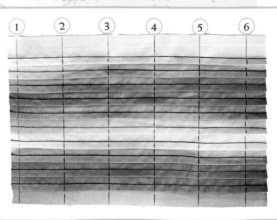

3. With the piece right-side up, mark a vertical line on the tucks ¼" from the fabric's left-hand edge. Subsequent vertical lines should be spaced every 1¼" or 1½" apart and should run perpendicular to the tucks.

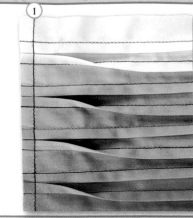

4. Working up vertical line 1, sew tucks 1 and 2 together by butting folds and using your sewing machine. Likewise, sew tucks 3 and 4 together. Continue sewing pairs together until the end of the line.

Do not machine stitch as photos illustrate. The stitch line is used to illustrate vertical pencil lines.

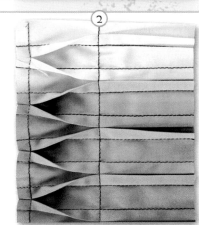

5. On vertical line 2, skip the first tuck and sew together tucks 2 and 3. Next, sew together tucks 4 and 5. To finish vertical line 2, continue sewing tucks together using this pattern.

Sew all remaining lines by alternating tuck pairs, as you did for Lines 1 and 2. For instance, you will sew together vertical line 3 just as you did vertical line 1. Line 4 will be exactly the same as 2.

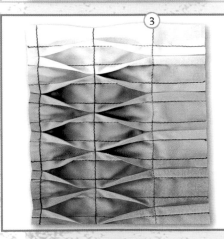

6. To embellish harlequin tucks, add beads where the tuck pairs are stitched together. Harlequin-tucked fabric pieces can be cut into any shape. Mark the desired shape on the right side of your fabric. Stitch along the marked lines, and be sure to cut just outside the lines to prevent the tucks from being undone. ✦

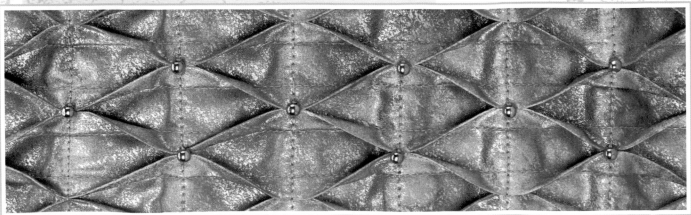

Pinwheels have always reminded me of my first bicycle. It was hot pink with ribbons to spare and covered in pinwheels, which I had folded from all sorts of colorful paper. As you can see from my pouch, a pinwheel is never out of place. Use this 3-D Ultrasuede Pinwheel to brighten your next project whether it has two pockets or two wheels.

1. Cut a square the desired size of the finished pinwheel. I used 1½" squares for my vest and pouch.

Fold the square in half diagonally. Finger press the fold, then open the piece. Fold the square in half diagonally in the opposite direction. Again, finger press then open the piece. The square will be creased with an X, as shown in the illustration. From each corner of the square, cut along the X, stopping ⅛" before the center.

2. Fold any point beyond the center of the X, as shown in the illustration. Repeat this fold at every other point as indicated.

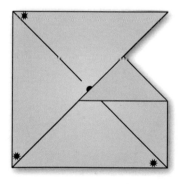

3. To anchor the points, make one stitch through the center of the pinwheel, sewing through all layers. Add a bead, crystal, or any other decorative embellishment to conceal the stitch. ✦

This silk wallhanging perfectly captures the versatility and simple elegance of Lotus Blossom Chopkey. For this project we will make three Lotus Blossoms, each in a different size. Please reference the cutting instructions below.

Fabric Requirements

Purple background	½ yd.
Gold background	fat quarter
Lotus Blossoms	
Dark gold	⅔ yd.
Khaki	⅜ yd.
Orange	fat quarter
Violet	fat quarter
Backing	½ yd.
Batting	½ yd.
Binding	¾ yd.

Cutting

	Small Circle	Medium Circle	Large Circle
Background circle diameter	11"	12½"	14"
after quilting, trim to	9"	10½"	12"
Square sizes for lotus blossom	3½" x 3½"	4" x 4"	4½" x 4½"
Number of squares to	dark gold 12	orange 8	dark gold 24
cut from each color	khaki 12	khaki 8	
		violet 8	

First, cut the background fabric, the batting, and the backing circle for each Lotus Blossom background. To accentuate my wallhanging, I chose to quilt the circles in a ½" diagonal grid using gold metallic thread. Trim each circle to the finished size then bind the edges.

Cut each Lotus Blossom petal square to its specified size. You will find the instructions on how to make the petals on pages 8–10.

Small Circle:

Attach the Lotus Blossom petals with beads positioned as shown in the photo.

Medium Circle:

With the Lotus Blossom right side up, fold the top point down beyond the inner edge of the circle, as shown in the photo. Attach each point with a bead, sewing through all the layers.

Large Circle:

Flip the Lotus Blossom over. To attach the flower, sew beads on the outer and inner points of the circle, sewing through all layers.

Make a hanger for the three circles using something stylish, such as a chain or ribbon. ✦

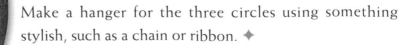

This Pillow Tote is a great way to wear your creativity. The smocked center inset lends this bag a style all its own, but an interesting fashion fabric could also be substituted for this section.

Fabric Requirements

Fashion fabric	½ yd.
Fabric for smocking	1⅝ yds.
Lining	⅔ yd.
Trim	3 yds.
Lotus Blossoms	2 fat quarters or assorted scraps
Zipper	14"

1. For the smocked pattern insert, cut your fabric 12" x 57". I recommend using a tone-on-tone or solid fabric to complement the elegant threading.

Mark a ½" grid of dots along the wrong side of the fabric. Comprehensive instructions for smocking, pattern 1, can be found on pages 24–25. Your finished piece will be 4½" x 25".

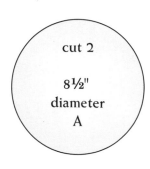

cut 2

8½" diameter
A

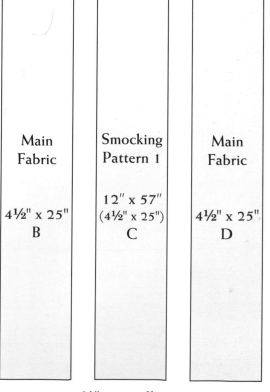

Main Fabric

4½" x 25"
B

Smocking Pattern 1

12" x 57"
(4½" x 25")
C

Main Fabric

4½" x 25"
D

use ¼" seam allowance

Cut your remaining fabric pieces, as shown in the illustration on page 39. Use a ¼″ seam allowance to join pieces B, C, and D. The sewn piece will be 12½″ x 25″. For added embellishment, insert trims into the seams between sections.

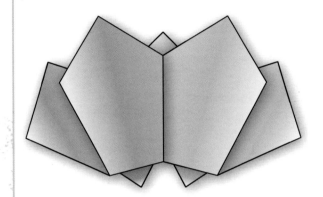

2. Install a zipper on the top and bottom edge of the sewn piece. To make two Lotus Blossoms for the circular side pieces, cut squares 3½″ and follow the folding instructions on pages 8–10.

Attach the Lotus Blossoms to two circular side pieces using beads.

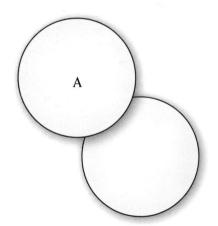

Sew pieces A (the side circles) to the pieced tote body. Again, for added embellishment, insert trims into the seams.

To make the bag lining, cut two circles and a 12½″ x 25″ rectangle. Sew circles onto the ends as you did for the bag but do not install a zipper.

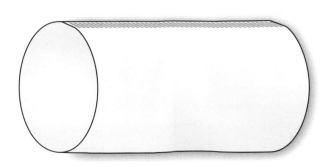

To hold the pillow tote bag's shape, sandwich batting and heavyweight interfacing between the outer bag and the lining. Install handles of your choice. ✦

ROMANCE. *Romance was inspired by light feelings of spring, after the gray winter is retired and nature begins its annual symphony. Flowers bloom and birds sing. True to those feelings, this project was a labor of love. Just marking the dots on the wrong side of the fabric, two yards of 45" wide silk dupioni, took me a whole week. To smock the piece by hand took me another three weeks.*

Add serenity to your dinner table with the Lotus Blossom Table Runner and Charger.

Large charger
15" diameter

Fabric Requirements

Table runner	½ yd.
Lining for table runner	½ yd.
Trim	3¾ yds.
Large charger	1 yd.
Small charger	¾ yd.

1. Cut 2 rectangles 14" x 54" from table runner fabric. Trim table runner ends as illustrated in the diagram.

2. With the right sides together, sew around the perimeter using a ½" seam allowance, be sure to leave an 8" to 10" opening. Turn the table runner right side out through the opening and then use a blind stitch to close the opening. If you want to embellish the runner, insert trim into the seams, or, after finishing the runner, add trim by topstitching it in place.

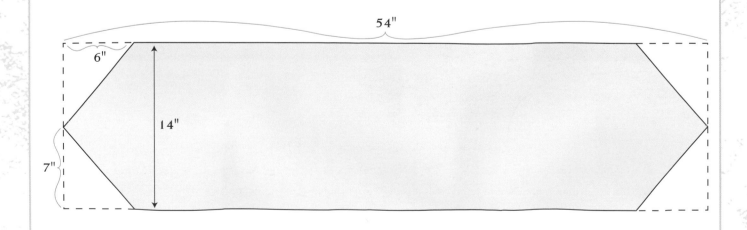

54"

6"

14"

7"

3. For the large charger, cut twenty-four 7" squares. Make Lotus Blossoms following the instructions on pages 8–10.

For the small charger, cut twenty-four 6" squares.

Stack the chargers on the table runner for a beautiful dining room table display. ✦

Small charger
12½" diameter

Inspiration Piece: KOI POND. *Koi are not only beautiful fish, but throughout Asian culture they have come to symbolize love, friendship, and perseverance. This sample is from a workshop I've been teaching. Using a bobbin-work technique, I depicted koi using a combination of fuzzy, sparkling yarns. Then, I added the three-dimensional Lotus Blossoms to the pond-shaped background.*

As you can see, the gentle Lotus Blossoms perfectly complement the sleek, angular hexagons, melding this wall-hanging into a symphony of contrasting shapes and colors. This charming piece is assembled using an easy, quilt-as-you-go method.

Fabric Requirements

5 Background squares	9½" x 9½" assorted colors
Inner border, triangle & binding	1 yd.
Lotus Blossoms	6" x 18" rectangles of
18 assorted colors (3 fabrics for each blossom)	
Hexagon Chopkey	45 assorted 5" squares
Accent bias border	fat quarter
Backing	1½ yd.
Batting	1½ yd.

1. Cut five 9½" background squares, using five different colored fabrics.

Make a long strip by sewing the squares together using a ¼" seam allowance.

Cut both your batting and backing 25" x 65". Layer the batting on top of the backing, wrong sides up, and then add the strip of squares right side up. The strip should be centered between the left and right edges of the batting, and 4" below the top edge, as shown in the illustration.

Baste the layers. Quilt the five blocks using a pattern of your choice, for example, free-motion stippling or diagonal grid quilting.

For the inner border, cut two strips 2"x 45½" and two strips 2"x 12½". Attach the long inner border strips to the sides of the five-block unit using a ¼" seam allowance and sewing through all the layers. Attach the top and bottom inner borders using a ¼" seam allowance.

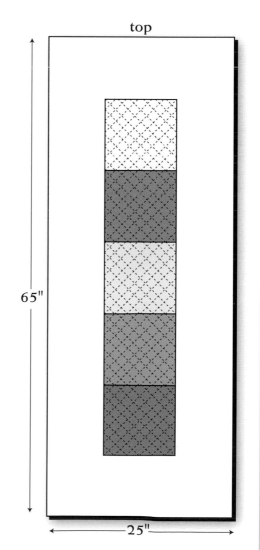

top

65"

25"

2. Using the template on page 49 (instructions on pages 11–13), make 48 Hexagon Chopkey in all different colors. To make a long chopkey ribbon, sew 24 hexagons together. Cut off the pointed sides of the strips by aligning your ruler along the inside corners. You will need two strips.

Butt the hexagon strips against the side borders. Baste them ⅛" from the raw edge. This will leave the raw edges exposed between the hexagons and the inner border.

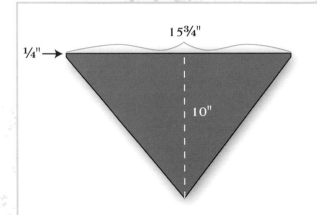

15¾"

¼" →

10"

3. Cut two strips 1" x 48½", and fold under ¼" on both long sides of each strip. To simplify this step, you can use a ½" bias tape maker. Cover the raw edges of the Hexagon Chopkey strips and side inner borders with the folded strips and topstitch in place.

Cut the bottom triangle, as shown in the illustration.

4. Sew the triangle to the bottom edge of the quilted squares using a ¼" seam allowance. Quilt the triangle with the quilting design of your choice.

Trim the batting and the backing so that they are even with the edges of the pieced unit. Bind your quilt with strips from an appropriate accent fabric.

Make six Lotus Blossoms using 4" x 4" squares. Instructions can be found on pages 8–10. Use beads to attach a Lotus Blossom to the center of each square. ✦

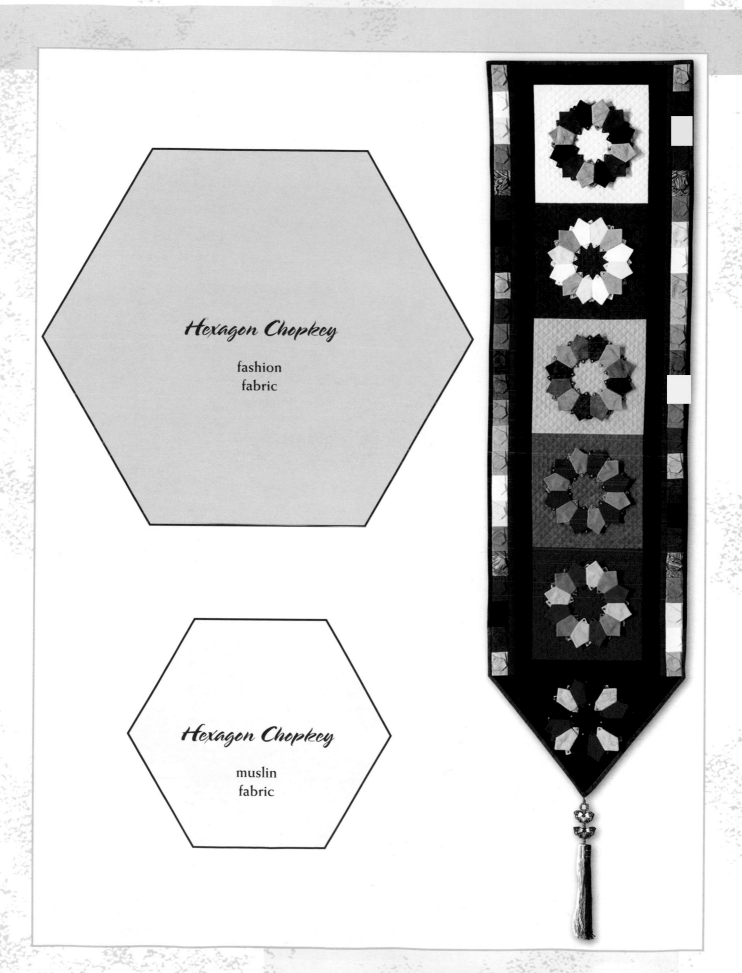

Hexagon Chopkey

fashion
fabric

Hexagon Chopkey

muslin
fabric

TWILIGHT IN SONOMA

This ensemble was inspired by the spectacular twilights of Sonoma County, California. To capture the enchanting colors and specific feelings of that special time of day, I used batik cottons, metallic threads, and of course Chopkey Hexagons. TWILIGHT IN SONOMA won first place at the 1999 International Quilt Week in Yokohama, Japan.

GUACAMOLISH. *Inspired by all the colors in guacamole, one of my favorite dips, I created this garment. Silk dupioni and silks from Korea added beautiful shine to the garment, and three-dimensional textures, like smocking and Hexagon Chopkey, added more interest.* GUACAMOLISH *won first place at the 2004 Pennsylvania Quilt Extravaganza.*

Beautiful and elegant, this pillow will enhance any room. These instructions are for an 18" pillow.

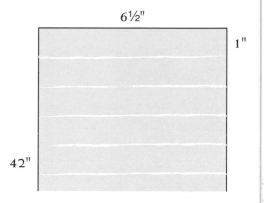

1. Cut a 6½" x 42" piece of fabric for the tucked center portion of the pillow. Use either a tone-on-tone or solid fabric. Mark 1" vertical lines along the right side of the fabric with an erasable marker, such as chalk.

2. With the right side up, fold the fabric with wrong sides together at the first marked line and press to crease. Open the fold. Fold and press each subsequent line. Make tucks by sewing along each line ¼" from the fold. Press the tucks all one direction.

Sew the two long edges using a ¼" seam allowance. Be sure to follow the direction of the tucks.

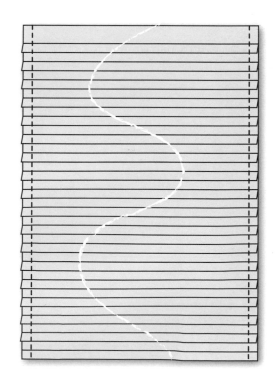

3. Using an erasable marker such as chalk, draw a curvy line down the center of the tucks, as shown in the illustration. Following along this line, stitch each tuck in the opposite direction from which it was originally pressed then gently steam press to set the curves. Embellish the tucks with beads.

	Hexagon Chopkey	2" x 18½" main fabric			
4½" x 18½" main fabric			5½" x 18½" tucked		

Trim the tucked piece to 5½" x 18½". Cut two 2" x 18½" strips from the main fabric. Sew a strip to each side of the tucked piece using a ¼" seam allowance.

4. Make two Hexagon Chopkey strips following the directions on pages 11–13. Each strip should have ten hexagon units. Trim each strip to 1¾" x 18½". Sew a strip to each long side of the piece using a ¼" seam allowance.

5. To complete the pillow top, cut two 4¼" x 18½" strips from the main fabric, and sew a strip to each long side using a ¼" seam allowance.

Add tassel trim if desired.

6. Cut an 18½" square from the main fabric to be used for backing. Layer the pieces right sides together. Leaving one side open, sew around the perimeter using a ½" seam allowance. Insert rope trim in-between seams.

Turn the pillow right side out and insert an 18" pillow form through the opening. Blind stitch the opening closed. ✦

HEXAGON CHOPKEY VEST

I painted these silks in one of Yvonne Porcella's silk-painting workshops some years ago. I made Hexagon Chopkey motifs from those silks and included lined prairie points to add a three-dimensional texture to the strip-pieced background. The vest pattern is my original design.

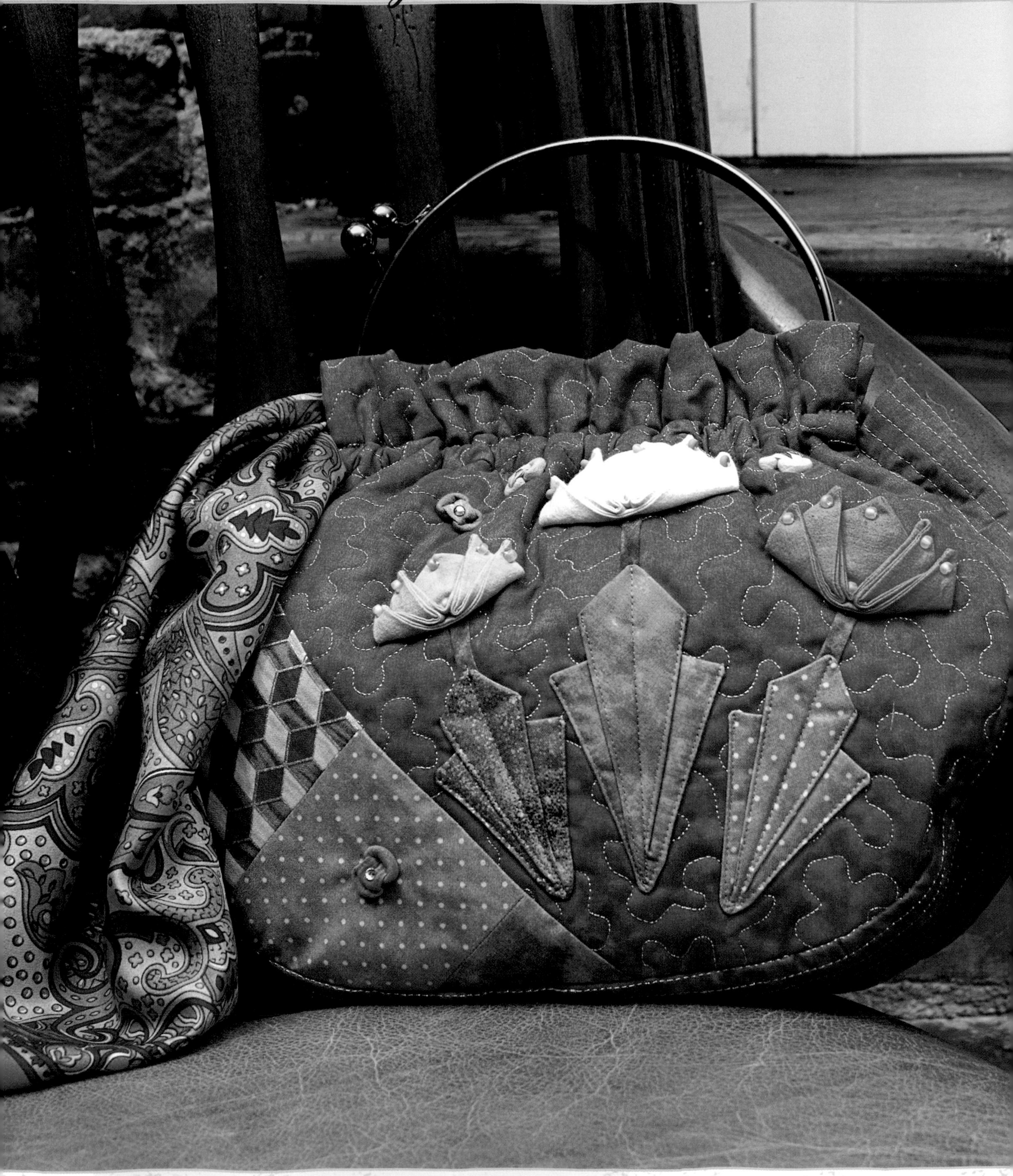

Whether you want a touch of fashion or a taste of spring, this darling purse is a perfect way to enjoy both.

Fabric Requirements

Fashion fabric	¾ yd.
Lining	¾ yd.
5 rectangles 3½" x 5" in assorted colors	
Assorted scraps for tulips, leaves, and lightning bugs	
Purse handles	

1. Using the bag pattern on page 60, cut two pieces of your background fabric and two pieces of batting.

Lay one piece of background fabric right-side-up on one piece of batting. Quilt the two layers in a pattern of your choosing, such as free-motion stippling or diagonal grid. Repeat this step with your second piece of background fabric and batting.

To decorate the bag front, cut four 3½" x 5" rectangles in different fabrics. Sew them together along their long sides to form a unit, as shown in the illustration.

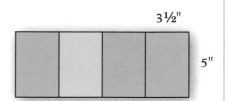

3½"

5"

2. Sew the rectangle unit diagonally across the bag's front, as shown in the illlustration. Trim the unit to the shape of the bag.

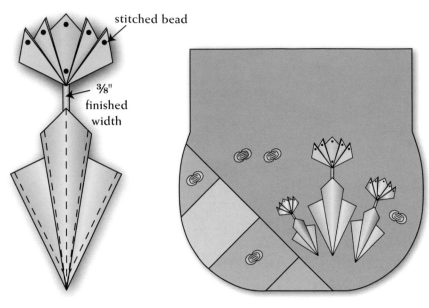

stitched bead

⅜"
finished
width

Make three Asheeya Tulips in different sizes using the instructions found on pages 14–17. Attach the flowers to the bag with beads. Topstitch the leaves onto the bag.

3. Make five or six lightning bugs using the instructions found on pages 18–19. You should use squares between 2½" to 3". Stitch the lightning bugs onto the front of the bag.

4. Using the bag pattern on page 60, cut two lining pieces. Place the front piece and one piece of lining with their right sides together. Sew around the perimeter using a ¼" seam allowance, leaving a 5" opening at the top.

Turn the piece right side out and press. Using a slipstitch, close the opening. Repeat this step for the bag's back, as shown in the illllustration.

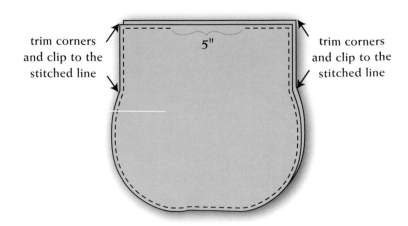

trim corners
and clip to the
stitched line

5"

trim corners
and clip to the
stitched line

5. Using the pattern on page 60, cut the background, batting, and lining for the side panel. Quilt the background and batting layers together, stitching straight lines ⅜" apart as illustrated.

6. With right sides together, sew the lining to the quilted side panel using a ¼" seam allowance, as shown in the illustration. Be sure to leave a 4" opening in the middle.

    Trim the corners and turn the side panel right side out. Press the panel. Close the opening using a slipstitch.

7. Whipstitch the front and back pieces to the side panel. Be sure to make the stitches on the fashion fabric, not the lining.

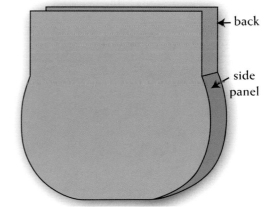

8. Fold down the top of the bag along the folding line, as indicated on the pattern. Stitch along the two casing lines on the front and back of the bag. This will make two casings for a metal frame.

    To insert a metal handle into the bag, unscrew the ball on rod end. Insert the rod through the bag casing. Once the handle is all the way through, screw the ball back onto the rod. Repeat the process with the other rod. Casings will gather because the rod is shorter than the casings. ✦

cut on fold

Tote Bag
Side Panel
side ¼" seam allowance included
cut 1 on fold with fashion fabric
cut 1 on fold with lining
cut 1 on fold with batting
enlarge pattern 200%

enlarge pattern 200%

fold line

two stitch lines for casing

casing

Tote Bag
Front & Back

cut 2 with fashion fabric
cut 2 with lining
cut 2 with batting

Rami Kim • Folded Fabric *Elegance*

WHEN BLUE BIRDS SING TO ME... *In April 1998, after a twelve year absence, I visited Seoul, South Korea. During the time I lived in Korea, I had been more interested in Levi's® jeans than Korean costumes, but during my trip I found myself rediscovering the exquisite hand embroideries found on traditional costumes called "Hanbok," that you might have seen in museums. When I returned home, I created this garment, an updated version of the garments worn during the Yi Dynasty. To capture that regal essence, I free-motion machine embroidered nearly 3,000 yards of thread, hand-beaded 1,000 beads, and free-motion stippled with Thermore® batting. You will notice the foundation-pieced curved Flying Geese are embellished with Continuous Prairie Points.*

This ensemble won Best of Show in the Hobbs Fashion Show and Contest at the 1999 AQS Show.

This Elegant Silk Bag is equally perfect for window shopping along Manhattan's Fifth Avenue or browsing your neighborhood quilt show.

Fabric Requirements

Black silk dupioni	½ yd.
Dark gold silk scrap	5" x 7"
Orange silk scrap	5" x 9"
Purple silk scrap	5" x 11"
Yellow silk scrap	5" x 7"
Yellow-green silk scrap	5" x 9"
Fuchsia silk	½ yd.
Lining	½ yd.
Batting	
Beads	
Handles	

Bag Back

1. Cut one 13" x 16" piece of black silk dupioni and one identically sized piece of batting. Layer the silk rectangle over the piece of batting and quilt together using a pattern of your choice, such as free-motion stippling or diagonal grid. I used a walking foot to quilt my bag with 45-degree diagonal lines spaced ½" apart.

Trim the piece to 11½" x 14½".

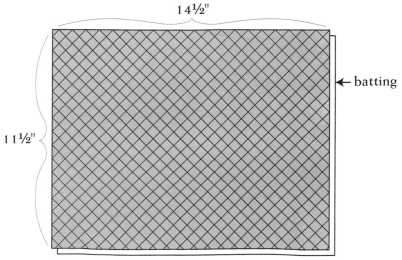

14½"

11½"

← batting

Bag Front

Finished sizes for the front sections.

1. Cut one 11" x 13" piece of black silk dupioni and one identically sized piece of batting. Layer the silk rectangle over the piece of batting and quilt together using straight lines spaced ⅜" apart.

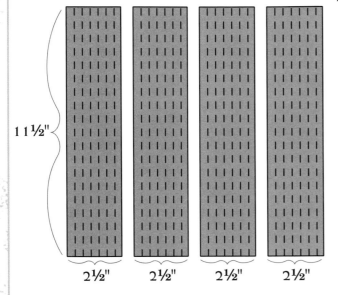

11½"

2½" 2½" 2½" 2½"

2. Cut the quilted piece into four 2½" x 11½" sections, as shown in the illustration.

3. Cut one 9" x 13" piece of black silk dupioni and an identically sized piece of batting. Layer the silk rectangle over the piece of batting and quilt using 45-degree diagonal lines spaced ½" apart.

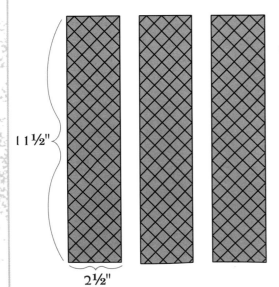

11½"

2½"

4. Cut the quilted piece into three 2½" x 11½" sections.

5. Make six different Continuous Prairie Points using six different fabrics. Cut your first two strips according to the illustration. Follow the Continuous Prairie Point instructions on pages 20–23. As you may notice in the bag pictured, I used purple for my right-sided strip and fuchsia for the left-sided strip.

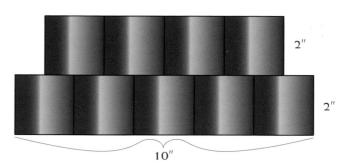

2"

2"

10"

6. Cut two strips 2 prairie points shorter, as in the illustration, and follow the Continuous Prairie Point instructions on pages 20–23. This will make the green right-sided and orange left-sided strips, as seen in the picture.

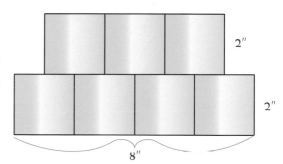

2"

2"

8"

7. Cut the last two strips 4 prairie points shorter, as in the illustration, and follow the Continuous Prairie Point instructions on pages 20–23 This will make the dark gold right-sided and yellow left-sided strips, as seen in the picture.

2"

2"

6"

8. Sew the seven bag front sections together, inserting the Continuous Prairie Point strips into the seams, as shown in the illustration. Press the seam allowances toward the center of the bag.

Poke a finger into each prairie point and spread it open. Add a bead or any other embellishment in the center by stitching through all the layers.

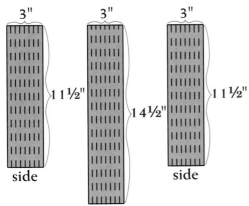

Bag Assembly

1. Using black silk and batting, prepare two quilted side pieces and one quilted bottom piece, as shown in the illustration.

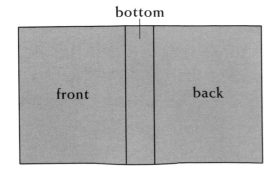

2. Sew the bag's front and back to the bottom piece using a ¼" seam allowance.

3. Sew the side pieces to the front, back, and bottom piece using a ¼" seam allowance.

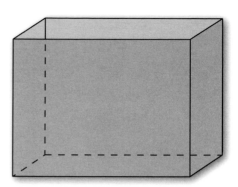

4. For the ruffle, cut two 5" x 45" strips of fuchsia silk dupioni then sew them together to form one 5" x 90" strip. Fold the strip in half lengthwise so that its dimensions are now 2½" x 90".

Gather a raw edge so that the strip fits the top of the bag, as shown in the illustration. Baste the gathered strip to the right side of the bag.

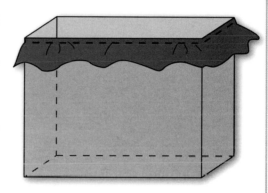

5. Make the lining by following the bag's cutting and assembly instructions.

Place the bag in the lining with right sides together. Stitch the top edge leaving an 8″ opening. Turn the bag right side out through the opening then slipstitch the gap closed.

Install handles of your choice. ✦

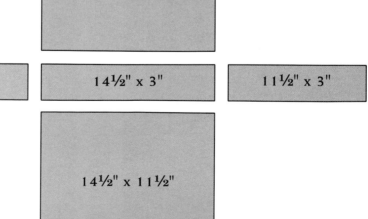

14½" x 11½"

11½" x 3"   14½" x 3"   11½" x 3"

14½" x 11½"

FASCINATION. *I labored for quite some time designing this piece. After it was finally finished, my very supportive husband laughingly told me, "You'd better do something with that garment since all I could see for two months was the back of your head facing your sewing machine."*

FASCINATION *won Best of Show at the 1997 Pacific International Quilt Festival, where I was lucky enough to be awarded a top of the line Bernina sewing machine and a nice amount of cash to buy some more fabrics. "Wow!" my husband exclaimed, hardly believing that his wife's hobby could actually make some money.*

The techniques used in FASCINATION *include: mirror-imaged, Continuous Prairie Points, curved Flying Geese, free-motion stippling, pin-tucking, Seminole patchwork, and hand beading.*

This pillow is fit for a queen. Its elegant embellishment might have you ringing for the servants if it weren't so fun to make. Instead, you'll be ruling over the sewing room in imperial fashion.

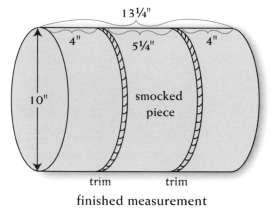

13¼"

4"   5¼"   4"

10"

smocked piece

trim   trim

finished measurement

Fabric Requirements

Textured inset	2⅓ yds.
Main fabric	1 yd.
Tassel trim	2 yds.
Rope trim	2 yds.
Bolster pillow form	

1. Cut two 5" X 32½" pieces of the main fabric.

Cut one 16" x 82" piece of coordinating, tone-on-tone fabric for smocking, pattern 1, pages 24–25.

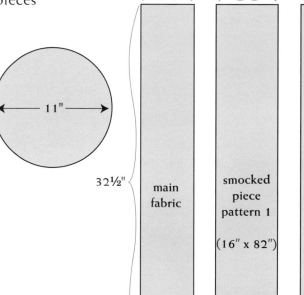
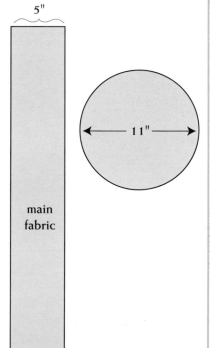

5"   6¼"   5"

11"   11"

32½"

main fabric

smocked piece pattern 1

(16" x 82")

main fabric

½" seam allowance included

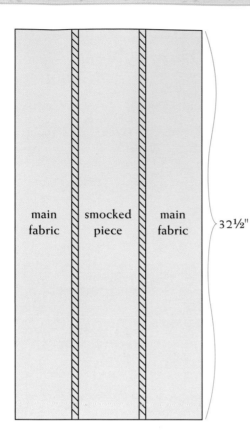

main fabric	smocked piece	main fabric

32½"

2. Mark a ½" grid of dots along the wrong side of the coordinating fabric. Hand smock the coordinating fabric using the instructions on pages 24–25. Trim the piece to 6¼" x 32½".

Sew together the two main fabric pieces and the smocked section to create a 14¼" x 32½" panel, as shown in the illustration. For added embellishment, insert a trim between the seams.

Sew the top and bottom edges of the panel and make it into a tube shape.

3. Cut two circles 11" in diameter. With right sides together, sew the circles to the panel leaving a 9" opening on one end. For added embellishment, topstitch trims onto the circles before stitching to the panel.

Turn right-side-out through the opening. Put a purchased bolster pillow form into the finished case and sew the gap closed. ✦

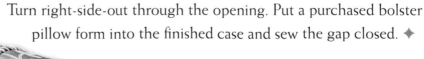

베개

REMINISCENCE. *This piece reminds me of my time in Korea. Like a true reminiscence, my memories are colored greatly by my experiences in the here-and-now. Equal parts Levi Strauss and Seoul, this piece won Best in Show at the 2005 Mid-Atlantic Wearable Art Festival.*

The background fabric is free-motion quilted with Hobbs Thermore® batting. North American smocking is used to enhance the texture. Some of the design is done using Bernina Embroidary Card #526, and the piece is finished off with my own embellishments including several of my own embroidery designs, silk ribbon embroidery, and beading.

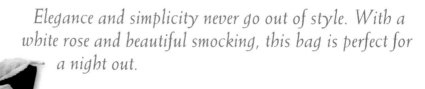

Elegance and simplicity never go out of style. With a white rose and beautiful smocking, this bag is perfect for a night out.

Fabric Requirements

Black	⅔ yd.
White	⅔ yd.
Lining	½ yd.
Batting	28½" x 14½"
Set of handles	
Silk flower	

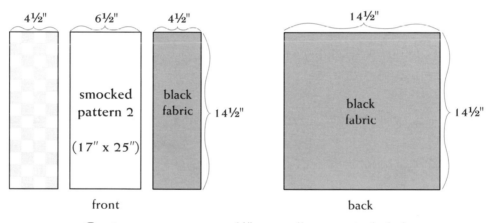

4½"   6½"   4½"   14½"

smocked pattern 2

(17" x 25")

black fabric   14½"

black fabric   14½"

front   back

Cutting measurements – ¼" seam allowance included

1. Cut one 17" x 25" piece of white fabric.

One the wrong side of the fabric and using a pencil, mark a grid and diagonal lines, as shown in the illustration.

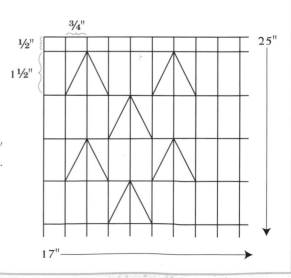

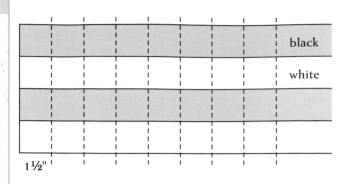

black

white

1½"

2. Machine smock the fabric piece using the pattern 2 instructions on pages 26–27. Trim the piece to 6½" x 14½".

Cut two 1½" x 24" strips of black fabric. Cut two 1½" x 24" strips of white fabric. To make a strip-set, sew the strips together lengthwise in an alternating pattern, as shown in the illustration.

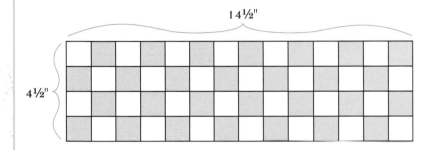

14½"

4½"

3. Cut the strip-set into fourteen 1½" segments. Sew the segments together to make a 4½" x 14½" checkerboard section.

4. Cut a 4½" x 14½" piece of black fabric. To make the bag front, sew together the checkerboard, smocking and black piece, as shown in the illustration.

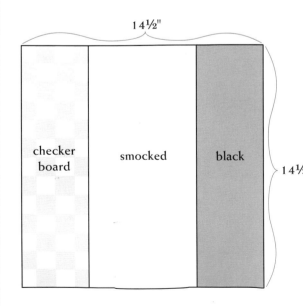

14½"

checker board

smocked

black

14½"

5. Cut a 14½" x 14½" piece of batting and place it under the bag front. Quilt the checkerboard and black sections.

Cut a 14½" x 14½" piece of black fabric and piece of batting the same size. To make the bag back, layer the two pieces and quilt. Sew the bag front and back together along the sides and bottom.

Sew a prepared lining to the bag following the conventional method.

Install handles of your choice. Embellish the purse with a silk rose. ✦

SECRET GARDEN. *A wise woman knows to stop wishing for things long enough to enjoy her blessings. My Secret Garden symbolizes those things I hold most dear: enchanting flowers, sunshine, my family, and my fondest memories.*

The colors of the iridescent silk dupioni vary depending on the angle from which they are seen. In fact, it is this fabric which single-handedly inspired me to play around with three-dimensional folding. SECRET GARDEN is embellished with Hexagon Chopkey and silk ribbon hand-embroidery. Even if I don't have a green thumb, my Secret Garden is filled with flowers that always bloom, brick pathways, and golden honeycombs. This garment won First Place and the Viewer's Choice awards in the 2005 Pacific International Quilt Festival.

Fabric Requirements

Assorted themed fabrics	34 pieces of 4" squares
Assorted tone-on-tone fabrics	6 pieces of 12" squares
Bias binding and 1" strips	1 yd.
Backing	½ yd.
Batting	16" x 36"

1. Choose a theme for your wallhanging and begin collecting some related fabrics. As you might have guessed, my theme was chocolate.

Cut a 16" x 36" piece of backing fabric and a piece of thin batting at the same size. With the backing wrong side up, place the batting on top of the fabric and hand baste the two layers together.

2. Cut several 4" squares from a variety of theme fabrics.

Cut several 12" squares from tone-on-tone fabrics. Smock the squares using pattern 1 and/or pattern 3 directions on pages 24–25 and 28–30. Trim the smocked pieces to 4" squares. Keep in mind that you will need a combined total of forty 4" squares.

Arrange all the 4" squares diagonally with edges butted across basted batting. Hand baste the squares in place.

3. Cut enough 1" crosswise grain strips and fold those into ½" strips by folding under ¼" on both lengthwise sides. To simplify the process, use a ½" bias tape maker. Cover the raw edges of the squares. Edge stitch the strips in place using invisible thread.

Trim the wallhanging to the desired shape. Finish the raw edges of the quilt using bias binding. ✦

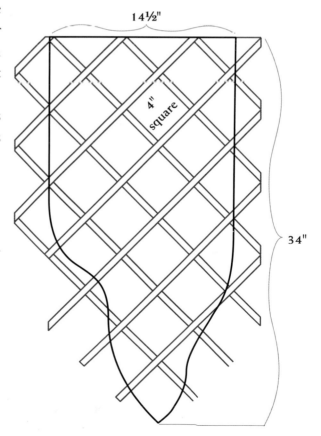

14½"

4" square

34"

CHOCOLATE. *I love chocolate, end of story, so when it came time to imagine a theme for this garment, I didn't have to think long or hard. Instead, it was right there on the tip of my tongue. To capture the dark silkiness of chocolate, I used a combination of silk dupioni, silk brocade, and cottons. The North American smocking, done by hand, adds unmistakable dimension to the piece. This garment also includes small-scale Harlequin Tucks, peyote-stitched beaded leaves, and more.*

CHOCOLATE won Best of Show as well as Viewers Choice at the 2003 Hobbs Fashion Show & Contest at the AQS Show.

Stay fashionable on your next trip to the park with this Harlequin Tuck Bag.

Fabric Requirements

Orange dots	½ yd.
Green dots	½ yd.
Orange/gold	¾ yd.
Lining	¾ yd.
Batting	40" x 27"
Handles	
Snaps	

1. Cut a 14" x 17" piece of orange fabric. Quilt the piece using a batting of your choice. Trim the piece to 13" x 16". Likewise, cut and quilt a 14" x 17" piece of yellow-green fabric. These pieces will be the front and back of the bag.

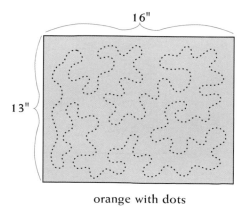

orange with dots

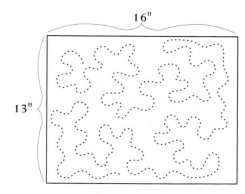

yellow-green with dots

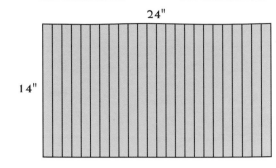

24"

14"

2. Cut a 24" x 14" piece of orange fabric. Make a Harlequin Tuck piece using the directions on pages 31–32. Trim the piece to 10" x 10". This piece will be the bag's front pocket.

3. Cut a 10" x 10" square of pocket lining. Layer the Harlequin piece and pocket lining with right sides together. Sew around three quarters of the piece using a ½" seam allowance, but leaving the bottom edge open. Turn the piece right-side-out.

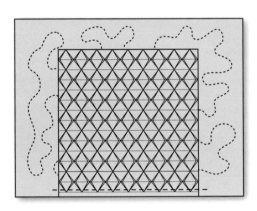

4. To stitch the lined pocket onto the quilted orange bag front, hand stitch two sides of the pocket and baste along the bottom, as shown in the illustration. A zipper can be hand sewn to the top edge if desired.

5. With right sides together, sew the bag front and back pieces together using a ½" seam allowance. Press the seam allowances open and topstitch along the seams.

6. Cut a 7" x 13" piece of either orange or yellow-green fabric to be used as the bag bottom. Quilt the piece using a batting of your choice. Cut the bag bottom from the quilted piece using the template on page 88.

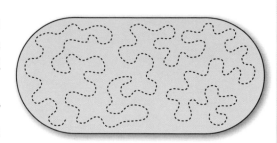

With right sides together, sew the bottom to the lower edge of the bag using a ½" seam allowance. Press the seam allowances toward the front and back pieces. Turn the bag right-side-out.

7. To make a lining, cut two 13" x 16" pieces to be used as the front and back. Cut a bottom piece using the pattern on page 88, then construct the lining.

With right sides together, sew together the upper edges of the lining and the bag, but leave a 7" opening. Turn the bag right-side-out through the gap.

8. Cut a piece of cardboard or very stiff interfacing by using the bag bottom pattern on page 88, but excluding the ½" seam allowance. Insert the cardboard bottom through the opening. It will hold the shape of the bag. Slipstitch the gap closed.

9. To shape the top of the bag like the one in the illustration, attach two tabs (1" x 2" finished size) to the upper sides and sew snaps on tabs. Install handles of your choice. ✦

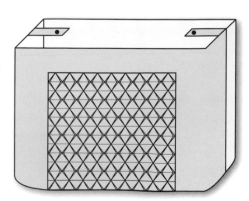

Harlequin Bag
Bottom

½" seam allowance included

cut on fold

POCAHONTAS 2001

My invitation to design a piece for the 2000 – 2001 Fairfield Fashion Show culminated into this garment, which is inspired by Hopi Indian designs. The Hopi frequently use white as a background for their designs to showcase their vibrant use of color and iconography. The Three-Dimensional Pinwheels add a lively, unexpected touch to the garment.

This stylish mini-pouch is the perfect accessory for quilters and fashion divas alike.

Fabric Requirements

4 assorted 8" x 10" rectangles	
Lining	¼ yd.
Batting	8" x 40" rectangle
Cording (loops)	¼ yd.
Ribbon (ties)	1½ yds.
Utrasuede scraps (pinwheels)	
Beads	

1. Cut four fabric pieces using the pattern on page 93.

Sew the four pieces together using a ¼" seam allowance, as shown in the illustration. Press the seam allowances open. If desired, quilt the pouch with layers of batting.

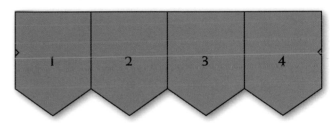

2. Cut 1¼" squares to be used to make pinwheels (cut as many as desired). Construct the pinwheels using the instructions on page 33. Anchor the pinwheels to the pouch wherever desired using beads, buttons, or another decorative embellishment to hide the stitch.

Sew the pouch together by stitching together the remaining seams between pieces 1 and 4. Press open the seam allowances. With right sides together, sew bottom seams A and B together, as shown in the illustration. Press open the seam allowances.

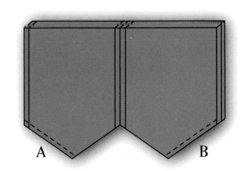

3. Sew the last bottom seam as shown.

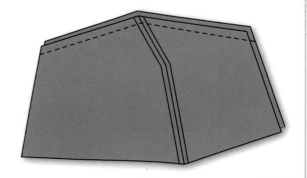

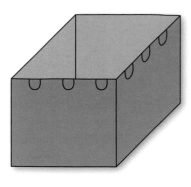

4. If a loop closure is desired, pin loops to the right side of the pouch as shown in the illustration.

Cut four lining pieces using the pattern on page 93. Use the pouch assembly instructions to make a lining.

With right sides together, sew the lining to the top of the pouch leaving a 3" opening. Turn the pouch right side out through the opening. Slip stitch the opening closed. Insert two drawstrings into the loops. ✦

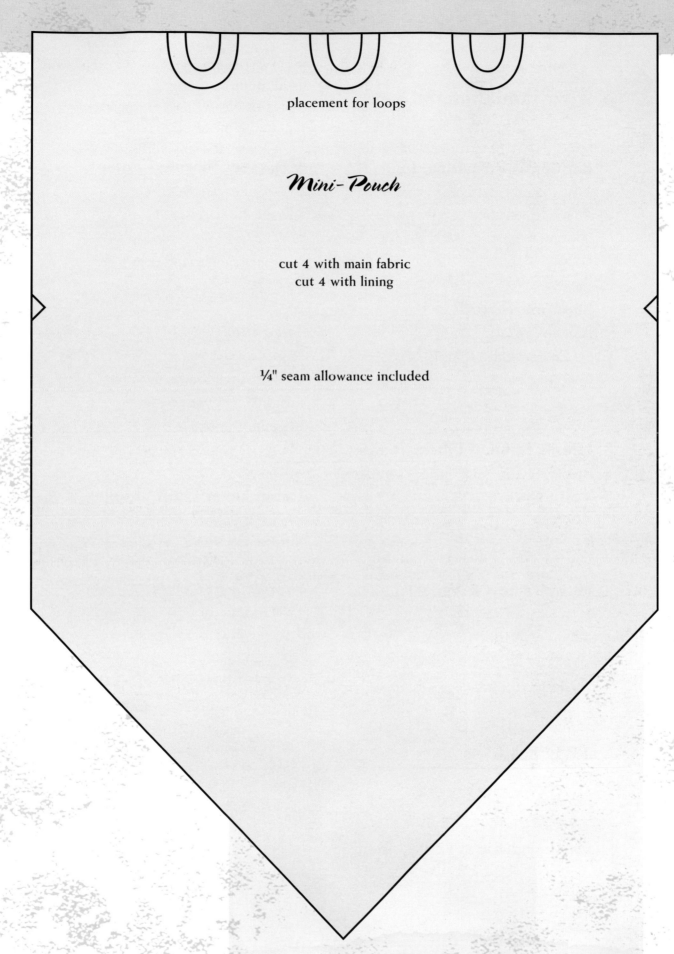

placement for loops

Mini-Pouch

cut 4 with main fabric
cut 4 with lining

¼" seam allowance included

Resources

www.ramikim.com

Bernina® of America, Inc.
3702 Prairie Lake Court
Aurora, IL 60504
(630) 978-2500

Superior Threads
P.O. Box 1672
St. George, UT 84771-1672
(435) 652-1867

Hobbs Bonded Fibers (batting)
P.O. 2521
Waco, TX 76702-2521
1-800-433-3357

Howell's Sew & Vac
2334 Grass Valley Hwy
Auburn, CA 95603
(530) 885-9624
www.howellsew.com

TWE/ Beads
P.O. Box 55
Hamburg, NJ 07419-0055
973-209-1517
www.twebeads.com

Meissner's Sewing Center
2417 Cormorant Way
Sacramento, CA 95815
1-800-521-2332
www.meissnersewing.com

Triad Plus
Fabrics for the Home
8801 Washington Blvd, Suite 107
Roseville, CA 95678
triadplus@hotmail.com

Cabin Fever Quilt Shoppe
826 Lincoln Way
Auburn, CA 95603
(530) 885-5500
www.cabinfeverquiltshoppe.com

자원

Rami Kim is a DNA scientist who turned in her lab coat to become a fabric artist, quilter, and international teacher. She graduated from Seoul National University and the University of California in San Francisco with degrees in chemistry and molecular endocrinology. She then put her scientific talent to work for the Cancer Research Institute at the University of California before her passion and talent in fabric art drastically changed this successful biochemist's career.

Presently the winner of 11 Best of Show awards as well as many other accolades, she has distinguished herself as an innovative and talented fabric artist. Her passion for contemporary art-to-wear, quilts, cloth dolls, bags, and one-of-a-kind home décor designs have won her international recognition. It is her distinctive use of 3-dimensional textures and color and unique interpretation of traditional sewing techniques that give her work an exquisite and fascinating edge.

Rami travels nationally and internationally and has appeared on HGTV's *Simply Quilts*, sharing her love of fabrics, thread, and technique along with her mega talent for putting them all together. When not traveling she lives with her husband and two daughters in California.

More AQS Books

This is only a small selection of the books available from the American Quilter's Society. AQS books are known worldwide for timely topics, clear writing, beautiful color photos, and accurate illustrations and patterns. The following books are available from your local bookseller, quilt shop, or public library.

#7018   us$24.95

#7490   us$22.95

#7487   us$19.95

#7491   us$22.95

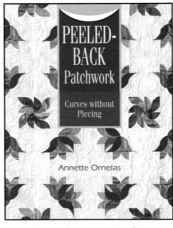

#6516   us$21.95

#7486   us$19.95

#7489   us$24.95

#7484   us$22.95

#7078   us$24.95

Look for these books nationally.
Call or **Visit** our Web site at

1-800-626-5420
www.AmericanQuilter.com